Das Lied von der Erde

IN FULL SCORE

Das Lied von der Erde

IN FULL SCORE

Gustav Mahler

Dover Publications, Inc., New York

This Dover edition, first published in 1988, is a republication of *Das Lied von der Erde: Eine Symphonie für eine Tenor- und eine Alt- (oder Bariton-) Stimme und Orchester (nach Hans Bethges "Die chinesische Flöte")*, originally published by Universal-Edition, Vienna, in 1912. A list of instruments in English, a glossary of German musical terms, and a new English translation of the texts have been added.

Manufactured in the United States of America
Dover Publications, Inc., 31 East 2nd Street, Mineola, N.Y. 11501.

Library of Congress Cataloging-in-Publication Data

Mahler, Gustav, 1860–1911.
  Das Lied von der Erde.

  Song cycle.
  For alto (or baritone), tenor, and orchestra.
  Text is a German translation by Bethge, in part expanded by Mahler, of Chinese poems.
  Originally published: Vienna : Universal Edition, 1912.
  Includes texts with English translations.
  1. Song cycles. 2. Songs (High voice) with orchestra—Scores. 3. Songs (Medium voice) with orchestra—Scores. 4. Songs (Low voice) with orchestra—Scores. I. Title.
M1613.M212L45   1988   87-754746
ISBN 0-486-25657-X

Contents

Instruments and Voices

Piccolo [kleine Flöte, kl. Fl.]
3 Flutes [Flöte, Fl.] (Fl. III alternates on Piccolo)
3 Oboes [Ob.] (Ob. I alternates on English Horn
      [Englisch Horn, Engl. Hr.])
E♭ Clarinet [Klarinette in Es, Kl. in Es]
3 B♭ Clarinets [Klarinette in B, Kl. in B]
Bass Clarinet [Bass-Klarinette, B. Kl.] (B♭, A)
3 Bassoons [Fagott, Fag.] (Bsn. III alternates on
      Contrabassoon [Kontra-Fagott, Kfag.]) (B♭, A)

4 Horns [Hn.] (F)
3 Trumpets [Trompete, Trp.] (F, B♭)
3 Trombones [Posaune, Pos.]
Tuba [Basstuba, Btb.]

Timpani [Pauken, Pk.]
Celesta [Cel.]
Mandolin [Mandol.]
Glockenspiel [Glocksp.]
Triangle [Triangel, Trgl.]
Bass Drum [grosse Trommel, gr. Tr.]
Cymbals [Becken, Beck.]
Tam-tam
Tambourine [Tamburin]

2 Harps [Harfe, Hfe.]

Violins I, II [Violine, Vl.]
Violas [Bratsche, Br.]
Cellos [Violoncell, Vlc.]
Basses [Kontrabass, Kb.]

Tenor [Tenor-Stimme, Ten.-St.]
Alto [Alt-Stimme, Alt-St.] or Baritone

Das Lied von der Erde.

I. Das Trinklied vom Jammer der Erde.

Schon winkt der Wein im gold'nen Pokale,
Doch trinkt noch nicht, erst sing' ich euch ein Lied!
Das Lied vom Kummer soll auflachend in die Seele euch klingen.
Wenn der Kummer naht, liegen wüst die Gärten der Seele,
Welkt hin und stirbt die Freude, der Gesang.
Dunkel ist das Leben, ist der Tod.

Herr dieses Hauses!
Dein Keller birgt die Fülle des goldenen Weins!
Hier, diese Laute nenn' ich mein!
Die Laute schlagen und die Gläser leeren,
Das sind die Dinge, die zusammen passen.
Ein voller Becher Weins zur rechten Zeit
Ist mehr wert, als alle Reiche dieser Erde!
Dunkel ist das Leben, ist der Tod.

Das Firmament blaut ewig und die Erde
Wird lange fest steh'n und aufblüh'n im Lenz.
Du aber, Mensch, wie lang lebst denn du?
Nicht hundert Jahre darfst du dich ergötzen
An all dem morschen Tande dieser Erde!
Seht dort hinab! Im Mondschein auf den Gräbern
Hockt eine wild-gespenstische Gestalt —
Ein Aff' ist's! Hört ihr, wie sein Heulen
Hinausgellt in den süßen Duft des Lebens!
Jetzt nehmt den Wein! Jetzt ist es Zeit, Genossen!
Leert eure gold'nen Becher zu Grund!
Dunkel ist das Leben, ist der Tod!

II. Der Einsame im Herbst.

Herbstnebel wallen bläulich überm See;
Vom Reif bezogen stehen alle Gräser;
Man meint, ein Künstler habe Staub von Jade
Über die feinen Blüten ausgestreut.

Der süße Duft der Blumen ist verflogen;
Ein kalter Wind beugt ihre Stengel nieder.
Bald werden die verwelkten, gold'nen Blätter
Der Lotosblüten auf dem Wasser zieh'n.

Mein Herz ist müde. Meine kleine Lampe
Erlosch mit Knistern, es gemahnt mich an den Schlaf,
Ich komm' zu dir, traute Ruhestätte!
Ja, gib mir Ruh', ich hab' Erquickung not!

Ich weine viel in meinen Einsamkeiten.
Der Herbst in meinem Herzen währt zu lange.
Sonne der Liebe willst du nie mehr scheinen,
Um meine bittern Tränen mild aufzutrocknen?

III. Von der Jugend.

Mitten in dem kleinen Teiche
Steht ein Pavillon aus grünem
Und aus weißem Porzellan.

Wie der Rücken eines Tigers
Wölbt die Brücke sich aus Jade
Zu dem Pavillon hinüber.

In dem Häuschen sitzen Freunde,
Schön gekleidet, trinken, plaudern,
Manche schreiben Verse nieder.

Ihre seidnen Ärmel gleiten
Rückwärts, ihre seidnen Mützen
Hocken lustig tief im Nacken.

Auf des kleinen Teiches stiller
Wasserfläche zeigt sich alles
Wunderlich im Spiegelbilde.

Alles auf dem Kopfe stehend
In dem Pavillon aus grünem
Und aus weißem Porzellan;

Wie ein Halbmond steht die Brücke,
Umgekehrt der Bogen. Freunde,
Schön gekleidet, trinken, plaudern.

IV. Von der Schönheit.

Junge Mädchen pflücken Blumen,
Pflücken Lotosblumen an dem Uferrande.
Zwischen Büschen und Blättern sitzen sie,
Sammeln Blüten in den Schoß und rufen
Sich einander Neckereien zu.
Gold'ne Sonne webt um die Gestalten,
Spiegelt sie im blanken Wasser wider,
Sonne spiegelt ihre schlanken Glieder,
Ihre süßen Augen wider,

Und der Zephir hebt mit Schmeichelkosen das Gewebe
Ihrer Ärmel auf, führt den Zauber
Ihrer Wohlgerüche durch die Luft.
O sieh, was tummeln sich für schöne Knaben
Dort an dem Uferrand auf mut'gen Rossen?
Weithin glänzend wie die Sonnenstrahlen;
Schon zwischen dem Geäst der grünen Weiden
Trabt das jungfrische Volk einher!
Das Roß des einen wiehert fröhlich auf
Und scheut und saust dahin,
Über Blumen, Gräser, wanken hin die Hufe,
Sie zerstampfen jäh im Sturm die hingesunk'nen Blüten,
Hei! Wie flattern im Taumel seine Mähnen,
Dampfen heiß die Nüstern!
Gold'ne Sonne webt um die Gestalten,
Spiegelt sie im blanken Wasser wider.
Und die schönste von den Jungfrau'n sendet
Lange Blicke ihm der Sehnsucht nach.
Ihre stolze Haltung ist nur Verstellung.
In dem Funkeln ihrer großen Augen,
In dem Dunkel ihres heißen Blicks
Schwingt klagend noch die Erregung ihres Herzens nach

V. Der Trunkene im Frühling.

Wenn nur ein Traum das Leben ist,
Warum denn Müh' und Plag'!?
Ich trinke, bis ich nicht mehr kann,
Den ganzen, lieben Tag!

Und wenn ich nicht mehr trinken kann,
Weil Kehl' und Seele voll,
So tauml' ich bis zu meiner Tür
Und schlafe wundervoll!

Was hör' ich beim Erwachen? Horch!
Ein Vogel singt im Baum,
Ich frag' ihn, ob schon Frühling sei,
Mir ist als wie im Traum.

Der Vogel zwitschert: Ja!
Der Lenz ist da, sei kommen über Nacht!
Aus tiefstem Schauen lauscht' ich auf,
Der Vogel singt und lacht!

Ich fülle mir den Becher neu
Und leer' ihn bis zum Grund
Und singe, bis der Mond erglänzt
Am schwarzen Firmament!

Und wenn ich nicht mehr singen kann,
So schlaf' ich wieder ein,
Was geht mich denn der Frühling an!?
Laßt mich betrunken sein!

VI. Der Abschied.

Die Sonne scheidet hinter dem Gebirge
In alle Täler steigt der Abend nieder
Mit seinen Schatten, die voll Kühlung sind.
O sieh! Wie eine Silberbarke schwebt
Der Mond am blauen Himmelssee herauf.
Ich spüre eines feinen Windes Weh'n
Hinter den dunklen Fichten!
Der Bach singt voller Wohllaut durch das Dunkel.
Die Blumen blassen im Dämmerschein.
Die Erde atmet voll von Ruh' und Schlaf.
Alle Sehnsucht will nun träumen,
Die müden Menschen geh'n heimwärts,
Um im Schlaf vergess'nes Glück
Und Jugend neu zu lernen!
Die Vögel hocken still in ihren Zweigen
Die Welt schläft ein!
Es wehet kühl im Schatten meiner Fichten.
Ich stehe hier und harre meines Freundes;
Ich harre sein zum letzten Lebewohl.
Ich sehne mich, o Freund, an deiner Seite
Die Schönheit dieses Abends zu genießen.
Wo bleibst du? Du läßt mich lang allein!
Ich wandle auf und nieder mit meiner Laute
Auf Wegen, die vom weichen Grase schwellen.
O Schönheit! O ewigen Liebens — Lebens — trunk'ne Welt!
Er stieg vom Pferd und reichte ihm den Trunk
Des Abschieds dar. Er fragte ihn, wohin
Er führe und auch warum es müßte sein.
Er sprach, seine Stimme war umflort. Du, mein Freund,
Mir war auf dieser Welt das Glück nicht hold!
Wohin ich geh'? Ich geh', ich wand're in die Berge.
Ich suche Ruhe für mein einsam Herz.
Ich wandle nach der Heimat! Meiner Stätte.
Ich werde niemals in die Ferne schweifen.
Still ist mein Herz und harret seiner Stunde!
Die liebe Erde allüberall blüht auf im Lenz und grünt
Aufs neu! Allüberall und ewig blauen licht die Fernen!
Ewig . . . ewig . . .

The Song of the Earth

Texts adapted by Mahler from Hans Bethge's *Die chinesische Flöte*, a collection of free translations of Chinese poetry

I. The Drinking Song of the Sorrow of Earth

Already the wine beckons in the golden goblet,
But do not drink yet, first I will sing you all a song!
The song of trouble shall ring laughing in your soul.
When trouble nears, the gardens of the soul lie barren,
Joy and song wither away and die.
Dark is life, is death.

Master of this house!
Your cellar holds an abundance of golden wine!
Here, this lute I call mine!
To strike the lute and empty the glasses,
These are the things that go well together!
A full cup of wine at the right time
Is worth more than all the kingdoms of this earth!
Dark is life, is death.

The firmament shines blue forever and the earth
Will long endure and blossom forth in springtime.
But you, man, how long do you live?
Not a hundred years may you delight
In all the fragile trifles of this earth!
See down there! In the moonlight on the graves
Squats a wild ghostly form—
It is an ape! Hear how its howls
Shrill out into the sweet fragrance of life!
Now take the wine! Now it is time, comrades!
Empty your golden cups to the lees!
Dark is life, is death!   *After Li T'ai-po*

II. The Lonely One in Autumn

Autumn mists float blue over the lake;
Covered with frost are all the grasses;
It is as if an artist had sprinkled jade dust
Over the delicate blossoms.

The sweet odor of the flowers has vanished;
A cold wind bends down their stems.
Soon the wilted, golden leaves
Of the lotus blossoms will drift on the water.

My heart is weary. My little lamp
Has gone out with a sputter; I am put in mind of sleep.
I come to you, dear resting-place!
Yes, give me rest, I have need of refreshment!

I weep much in my times of loneliness.
The autumn in my heart persists too long.
Sun of love, will you shine no longer,
To gently dry my bitter tears?   *After Chang Tsi*

III. Of Youth

In the middle of the little pool
Stands a pavilion of green
And of white porcelain.

Like the back of a tiger
The bridge of jade arches
Over to the pavilion.

In the little house sit friends,
Beautifully dressed, drinking, chatting.
Some write down verses.

Their silken sleeves slip
Back, their silken caps
Perch comically low on their napes.

On the little pool's still
Surface everything appears
Wondrously in mirror image.

Everything standing on its head
In the pavilion of green
And of white porcelain.

Like a half-moon stands the bridge,
The arch inverted. Friends,
Beautifully dressed, drink, chat.   *After Li T'ai-po*

IV. Of Beauty

Young maidens pick flowers,
Pluck lotus blossoms on the bank.
Among bushes and leaves they sit,
Gather flowers in their laps and call
Bantering to each other.
Golden sun weaves about the forms,
Reflects them in the bright water,
Sun mirrors their slender limbs,
Their charming eyes,

And the zephyr with caresses lifts the fabric
Of their sleeves, carries the magic
Of their perfumes through the air.
Oh see, what handsome youths romp
There on the bank on spirited steeds?
In the distance they gleam like the sunbeams;
Now between the branches of the green willows
The vigorous lads trot along.
The horse of one neighs merrily
And shies and gallops off,
Over flowers, grasses, its hooves stagger,
Recklessly and stormily they trample the fallen flowers!
Ah! How its mane waves in frenzy,
Its nostrils steam hotly!
Golden sun weaves about the forms,
Reflects them in the bright water.
And the most beautiful of the virgins casts
Long glances of desire after him.
Her proud bearing is only pretense.
In the flashing of her large eyes,
In the darkness of her burning glance,
The agitation of her heart still trembles in lament.   *After Li T'ai-po*

V. The Drunkard in Spring

If life is only a dream,
Why then trouble and care?
I drink until I can drink no more,
The whole day long!

And when I can drink no more,
Because throat and soul are full,
Then I stagger to my door
And sleep wonderfully!

What do I hear on waking? Hark!
A bird sings in the tree.
I ask it whether it is already spring,
It is like a dream to me.

The bird chirps, "Yes!
Springtime is here, it has come overnight!"
Lost in gazing, I suddenly took heed,
The bird sings and laughs!

I fill my cup again
And empty it to the dregs
And sing until the moon gleams
In the black heavens!

And when I can sing no more,
Then I fall asleep again.
What has the spring to do with me?
Let me be drunk!   *After Li T'ai-po*

VI. The Farewell

The sun departs behind the mountains.
Into all the valleys the evening descends
With its shadows, which are full of coolness.
Oh see! Like a silver barque
The moon floats upward on the blue lake of heaven.
I feel a soft wind blowing
Behind the dark spruces.
The brook sings, full of pleasant sound, through the dark.
The flowers pale in the twilight,
The earth breathes, full of quiet and sleep.
All longing now wants to dream.
Weary men go homeward,
To learn again in sleep
Forgotten happiness and youth.
The birds perch quietly in their branches,
The world falls asleep!
A cool breeze blows in the shade of my spruces.
I stand here and await my friend;
I await him for a final farewell.
I long, O friend, to enjoy
The beauty of this evening at your side.
Where are you? You leave me alone so long!
I walk up and down with my lute
On paths that swell with soft grass.
O beauty! O world drunk with eternal love and life!
He alighted from his horse and offered him the draught
Of farewell. He asked him where
He was bound and also why it had to be.
He spoke, his voice was veiled: My friend,
Fortune was not kind to me in this world!
Where do I go? I walk, I wander into the mountains.
I seek peace for my lonely heart.
I go to my homeland, my abode!
I will never roam in distant lands.
My heart is still and awaits its hour.
The beloved earth everywhere blossoms and greens in springtime
Anew. Everywhere and forever the distances brighten blue!
Forever . . . forever . . .

After Meng Kao-yen and Wang Wei

Glossary of German Musical Terms in the Score

ab, off; *aber*, but; *abreissen*, cut off; *Akkord*, chord; *alle*, all; *allmählich*, becoming gradually; *als*, as; *angegeben*, notated; *Anmerkung*, note; *auch*, also; *auf*, up, on; *Aufschwung*, impetus, drive; *Ausdruck*, expression; *ausdrucksvoll*, expressive; *auszuführen*, to be played; *b*, B♭; *Bariton*, baritone; *Bässe*, double basses; *behaglich*, comfortably; *bei*, on; *belebend*, growing lively; *besetzt*, played; *besitzt*, occupy, reach; *bewegter*, faster; *bezeichnet*, marked; *bis*, until; *blasen*, play; *bloss*, only; *Bogen*, bow; *brechen*, arpeggiate; *Dämpfer*, *Dämpf.*, mute(s); *das*, the; *decken*, cover, obscure; *die*, the; *diese*, this, these; *Dirigenten*, conductor; *Doppelgriff*, double stop; *drängend*, pressing, stringendo; *drängender*, more pressing; *dur*, major; *durchaus*, throughout; *düster*, mournful; *edel*, nobly; *eilen*, hurry; *einem*, a, *dem einen*, the single; *einzelne*, individual; *Empfindung*, feeling; *ermüdet*, weary; *ersten*, first; *ersterbend*, dying away; *erzählend*, in speaking style, *erzählendem*, narrative; *es*, it; *Es moll*, E♭ minor; *etwas*, somewhat; *eventuell*, if necessary; *Figuren*, figures; *Flageolet*, *Flag.*, harmonics; *Flatterzunge*, flutter-tongue; *fliessend*, flowing, *fliessender*, more flowing; *Flötist*, flutist; *flotter*, livelier; *für*, for; *ganz*, utterly, quite; *ganze*, whole; *gänzlich*, completely; *gebrochen*, broken, arpeggiated; *gegen*, compared to; *gehalten*, sostenuto, *gehaltener*, more sustained; *gerissen*, tearing, rending; *gestopft*, stopped; *gestrichen*, bowed; *gesungen*, sung; *geteilt*, *get.*, divisi, *3fach geteilt*, divisi in 3; *getragen*, solemn; *gis tief*, low G♯; *gleichmässig*, evenly; *glühend*, glowing; *(am) Griffbrett*, sul tasto; *grossem*, great, *grösstem*, the greatest; *h*, B; *halten*, hold; *heben*, raise; *heiter*, cheerful; *hervortretend*, prominent; *Holzschlägel*, wood mallets; *hörbar*, audible; *im*, in; *immer*, always, steadily; *innig*, heartfelt; *innigster*, the most heartfelt; *1.*, *2.*, *3.*, *4.*, 1st, 2nd, 3rd, 4th; *1ten*, first, *2ten*, second; *ist*, is; *jede*, each; *jedesmal*, always; *kann*, can; *kaum*, barely; *keck*, bold, brazen; *keinen*, no; *klingt*, sounds; *Kontra-C*, low C; *Kraft*, strength; *kurz*, short; *lang*, long, *so lange*, as long as, when, if; *langsam*, slow; *leidenschaftlich*, passionate, *leidenschaftlichstem*, the most passionate; *mag*, may; *marschmässig*, marchlike; *mässig*, moderato; *Mediator*, plectrum; *melodisch*, melodically; *mit*, with; *möglich*, possible; *muss*, must; *Nachahmung*, imitation; *nicht*, not, don't; *nimmt*, takes, changes to; *noch*, still; *Note*, note; *nur*, only; *oder*, or; *offen*, open; *ohne*, without; *Pausen*, rests; *pausieren*, tacet; *Pedalton*, pedal tone; *Pult*, desk, stand; *Resonanz.*, near the soundboard; *roh*, raw, coarse; *ruhig*, peaceful, *ruhiger*, more peaceful; *Saite*, string; *sanft*, gently; *Schalltrichter*, *Schalltr.*, bells (of wind instruments); *scharf*, sharply; *schauernd*, shivering; *schlagen*, beat; *schleichend*, lingering; *schleppen*, drag, *schleppend*, dragging, slow; *Schluss*, end; *schmeichelnd*, wheedling, caressing; *schnell*, fast; *Schwammschlegel*, sponge mallets; *schwer*, serious; *sehr*, very; *sein*, be; *sich beruhigend*, calm; *sinnend*, musing; *so*, as, then; *Spieler*, player; *spring. Bogen*, sautillé, saltando; *stark*, strongly; *statt*, instead of; *am Steg*, sul ponticello; *steigernd*, more intensely; *Steigerung*, intensifying; *stets*, always; *im Takt*, in time; *Takte*, bars; *Taktteil*, beat; *Ton*, tone, note; *Töne*, notes; *Tongebung*, tone; *tonlos*, toneless; *Triole*, triplets; *trotz*, despite; *übergehend*, progressing, proceeding; *übernimmt*, takes; *übernommen werden*, be taken, be sung; *die übrig.*, the rest, the others; *und*, and; *ungebrochen*, unarpeggiated; *verklingend*, fading away; *versehenen*, provided; *viel*, much; *voller*, full; *von*, by; *vor*, before; *vorher*, previously; *Vorschläge*, grace notes; *wechseln*, change; *weich*, tender; *wenn*, if; *wie*, as, like; *wieder*, again; *wild*, unrestrained; *zart*, *zärtlich*, gently, sensitively, subdued; *Zeichen*, symbol; *Zeit lassen*, allow time; *zögernd*, hesitating; *zu*, too, *zu 2, 3*, divisi in 2, 3, or unison; *zum*, to the; *Zungenstoss*, staccato tongue; *zurückhaltend*, held back, meno mosso; *zwei*, two.

Das Lied von der Erde

IN FULL SCORE

Das Lied von der Erde.

I. Das Trinklied vom Jammer der Erde.

14 Das Trinklied vom Jammer der Erde

24   Das Trinklied vom Jammer der Erde

34 Das Trinklied vom Jammer der Erde

II. Der Einsame im Herbst.

III. Von der Jugend.

IV. Von der Schönheit.

61

*) Diese Triole jedesmal mit spring. Bogen *rfz* am Steg (in Nachahmung der Mandolinen.)
**) Der Doppelgriff (oder Akkord) mit (bezeichnet ist stets unisono, nicht geteilt auszuführen.

*) Die Trompeten heben den Schalltrichter bloß bei dem einen Ton (gis tief) auf.

V. Der Trunkene im Frühling.

*) Alle Vorschläge vor dem Taktteil und so schnell als möglich.

VI. Der Abschied.

*) Bässe ohne Kontra-C pausieren.

*) Wenn der Flötist keinen großen Ton hat, so übernimmt die Oboe dieses Solo.
**) Die Alt-Stimme muß sehr zart sein und das Flöten-Solo nicht „decken".

NB. Anmerkung für den Dirigenten:
Ganze Takte sehr langsam schlagen.